SENT BY EARTH

THE OPEN MEDIA PAMPHLET SERIES

SENT BY EARTH

A Message from the Grandmother Spirit

After the Attacks on the World Trade Center and Pentagon

Alice Walker

SEVEN STORIES PRESS / New York

love is not concerned
with whom you pray
or where you slept
the night you ran away
from home

love is concerned
that the beating of your heart
the beating of your heart
should harm
no one

SENT BY EARTH
A MESSAGE FROM THE GRANDMOTHER SPIRIT

Adapted from a speech to the
Midwives Alliance of North America
Albuquerque, New Mexico
September 22, 2001

"The Great danger in the world today is that the very feeling and conception of what is a human being might well be lost."

—Richard Wright to Jean Paul Sartre (1940s)[1]

This is one of the epigrams I chose to preface my first novel, *The Third Life of Grange Copeland*, 1970, which was about the challenge of remaining human under the horrific conditions of American Apartheid in the Southern United States during my parents and grandparents' time. They and their children faced massively destructive psychological and physical violence from landowners who used every conceivable weapon to keep the sharecropping/slave labor system intact. It was a system in which a relatively few ruling class white people had the possibility of having as much food, land, space and cheap energy to run their enterprises as they wanted, while most people of color and many poor white people had barely enough of anything to keep themselves alive.

"We own our own souls, don't we?" is that novel's ringing central cry.

In my opinion, this is also the ringing central cry of our time.

I have been advised that there are several different groups of people in the audience; not just members of the Midwives Alliance of North America. I have been warned that some of these people are afraid I am just going to talk about birthin' and babies. However, I came to Albuquerque especially because I wish to be with Midwives, whose business of birthin' and babies is, I believe, the most honorable on earth.

A few days ago I was in the presence of Sobonfu Somé, a contemporary carrier of traditional, pre-colonial and perhaps pre-patriarchal, Ancient African life-ways. She taught us that in her culture, among the Dagara people of Burkina Faso, the most important thing that happens in a person's life is that they be welcomed when they are born. If they are not welcomed, all their lives they experience a feeling of not quite having arrived. There is anxiety. There is unease. This made me think of the title I had originally chosen for this talk, which changed after the bombing* of the World Trade Center and the Pentagon, "Seeing the Light; the Importance of Being Properly Born." Some of you who attended my talk last year may recall my story of my own birth: The midwife and my grandmother were present in the room, but alas, they were busy chatting by the fireplace as my mother, overwhelmed with pain, fainted as I was being born. Several minutes passed before they knew what had happened. Was the fire going out? I wonder,

---

* Planes were used as bombs.

even today. Were they busy, perhaps, restoring it? I realize that even at this late date I wish they'd been beside or on the bed, waiting to receive me, instead of halfway across the room. And that my mother had been conscious.

I wished this even more fervently after being permitted by a midwife friend to attend a home birth and to see for myself what is possible in terms of welcoming the newborn into its mother's arms, into the light of its father's smile, into the world and into its immediate community. (Fortunately, I grew up to understand I was, from the beginning, very welcomed by the universe.)

Sobonfu Somé then asked us to stand, as I am now asking you to do, and to turn to the person on either side, take their hands, look them in the eye, and tell them: I welcome you here. *Take your time doing this, there is no hurry. If this is a person you've never seen before in your life, so much the better.*

<hr />

Last January [more than ten years ago], when the war against Iraq was started, I was in Mexico writing a novel about a woman who is genitally mutilated in a ritual of female circumcision that her society imposes on all females. Genital mutilation is a mental and physical health hazard that directly affects some one hundred million women and girls worldwide, alive today, to whom it has been done. Because of increased risk of trauma during delivery, it affects the children to whom they give birth. Indirectly, because of its linkage to the spread of AIDS, especially among women and children, it affects the health and well-being of everyone on the planet.

With no television or radio, and no eagerness to see or hear arrogant Western males discussing their military prowess, their delight in their own "cleanhanded" destructiveness, I relied on a friend's phone calls to his son in San Francisco to keep me informed. His son told us about the huge resistance to the war in San Francisco, which made me love the city even more than I did already, and informed us too that he had been one of those demonstrators so outraged they'd closed down the Bay Bridge.

What to do? Go home and join the demonstrations, or continue to write about the fact that little girls' bodies are daily bombed by dull knives, rusty tin can tops and scissors, shards of unwashed glass—and that this is done to them not by a foreign power but by their own parents and societies? I decided to say put. To *continue this story—which became* Possessing The Secret Of Joy*—about female genital mutilation, a.k.a. female circumcision, which I believe is vital for the world to hear. But of course I could not forget the war being waged against the earth and the people of Iraq.*

Because I was thinking so hard about the suffering of little girls, while grieving over the frightened people trying to flee our government's bombs, my unconscious, in trying to help me balance my thoughts, did a quite wonderful thing. It gave me a substitute for Saddam Hussein, the solitary demon among tens of millions on whom the United States' military's bombs were falling. Her name was Sadie Hussein, and she was three years old. So, as the bombs fell, I thought about Sadie Hussein, with her bright dark eyes and chubby cheeks, her shiny black curls and her dainty pink dress, and I put my arms around her. I could not, however, save her.

As it turned out, this was the truth. Saddam Hussein still reigns, at least as secure in his power over the Iraqis, according to some media sources, as George Bush is over North Americans. It is Sadie Hussein who is being destroyed, and who, along with nine hundred thousand other Iraqi children under the age of five, is dying of cholera, malnutrition, infection, and diarrhea. Since the war, fifty thousand such children have died, It is Sadie Hussein who starves daily on less than half her body's nutritional needs, while Saddam Hussein actually appears to have gained weight.

This is the story of why I am here today. I am here because I pay taxes. More money in taxes in one year than my sharecropping parents, descendants of enslaved Africans and Indians, earned in a lifetime. My taxes helped pay for Sadie Hussein's suffering and death. The grief I feel about this will accompany me to my grave. I believe war is a weapon of persons without personal power, that is to say, the power to reason, the power to persuade, from a position of morality and integrity; and that to go to war with any enemy who is weaker than you is to admit you possess no resources within yourself to bring to bear on your own fate. I will think of George Bush vomiting once into the lap of the Japanese prime minister—and all the media considered this major news—and will immediately see hundreds of thousands of Iraqi children, cold, hungry, dying of fever, dysentery, typhoid, and every other sickness, vomiting endlessly into the laps of their mothers—who are also emaciated, starving, terrorized, and so illiterate they are unable to read Saddam Hussein's name, no matter how large he writes it.[2]

There is not a midwife in this room who would bomb a baby or a child or a pregnant woman. Perhaps in this particular room there is not one person who would do so. And yet, that is the position we find ourselves in. The war against Iraq continues. In the ten years since I wrote my lament, millions more have died, the majority of them small children. Unlike most North Americans I did not watch the initial bombing on television; I did see later, however, footage showing the bombing of a long line of what looked like old men trying to flee. They were running this way and that, their eyes filled with terror. I recognized more than I ever had that it is the very soul of the people of North America that is being lost, and that if this happens, for the rest of our time on the planet we are doomed to run with the dogs of war. The dogs of war. This is the vision that I have of this period. Ravenous, rapacious dogs, mad with greed and lust, red tongues out and salivating, running loose across the planet. They are the dogs that show up in some of the art of our time, in cartoons, or in the movie *Natural Born Killers*, by Oliver Stone. It is an ancient image, however, and what astonishes me is how accurately and irresistibly it has arisen in the psyche. And the psyche recognizes this image, not because it is only external. But because some part of it is internal as well. Which means we must all look inside and get to know our own dogs of war. Some of our war dogs, we have to own, are paying taxes that will be used to destroy people almost identical to us. Many of our war dogs are connected to heating our homes and driving cars.

A NATIVE PERSON LOOKS UP FROM THE PLATE
(Or, owning how we must look to a person
who has become our food.)

They are eating
us.
To step out of our doors
is to feel
their teeth
at our throats.

They are gobbling
up our
lands
our waters
our weavings
&
our artifacts.

They are nibbling
at the noses
of
our canoes
& moccasins.

They drink our oil
like cocktails
& lick down
our jewelry
like icicles.

They are siphoning
our songs.

They are devouring
us.
We brown, black
red and yellow,
unruly white
morsels
creating Life
until we die.
Spread out in the chilling sun
that is
their plate.

They are eating
us raw
without sauce.

Everywhere we
have been
we are no more.
Everywhere we are
going
they do not want.

They are eating
us whole.
The glint of their
teeth
the light
that beckons
us to table
where only they
will dine.

They are devouring
us.
Our histories.
Our heroes.
Our ancestors.
And all appetizing
youngsters
to come.

Where they graze
among
the people
who create
who labor
who live
in beauty
and walk
so lightly
on the earth
there is nothing
left.

Not even our roots
reminding us
to bloom.

Now they have wedged
the whole
of the earth
between their
cheeks.

Their
wide bellies
crazily clad
in stolen goods
are near
to bursting
with
the fine meal
gone foul
that is us.

Where do we start? How do we reclaim a proper relationship to the world?

It is said that in the Babemba tribe of South Africa, when a person acts irresponsibly or unjustly, he is placed in the center of the village, alone and unfettered.

All work ceases, and every man, woman and child in the village gathers in a large circle around the accused individual. Then each person in the tribe speaks to the accused, one at a time, about all the good things the person in the center of the circle has done in his lifetime. Every incident, every experience that can be recalled with any detail and accuracy is recounted. All his positive attributes, good deeds, strengths and kindnesses are recited carefully and at length.

The tribal ceremony often lasts several days. At the end, the tribal circle is broken, a joyous celebration takes place, and the person is symbolically and literally welcomed back into the tribe.

This will not be the fate of Osama bin Laden, accused of masterminding the attack on North America. In a war on Afghanistan, he will either be left alive, while thousands of impoverished, frightened people, most of them women and children and the elderly, are bombed into oblivion around him, or he will be killed in a bombing attack for which he seems, in his spirit—from what I have gleaned from news sources—quite prepared. In his mind, he is fighting a holy war against the United States. To die in battle against it would be an honor. He has been quoted as saying he would like to make the United States into a shadow of itself as he helped make the Soviet Union, which lost the war in Afghanistan, become a shadow of itself. In fact, he appears to take credit for helping the Soviet Union disintegrate. I personally would like him to understand that the shadow he wishes upon us, of poverty, fear, an almost constant state of terror, is merely the America too many of us already know. It is certainly the shadow my ancestors lived with for several hundred years.

But what would happen to his cool armor if he could be reminded of all the good, non-violent things he has done? Further, what would happen to him if he could be brought to understand the preciousness of the lives he has destroyed? This is not as simple a question as it might appear. I firmly believe the only punishment that works is love. Or, as the Buddha said: Hatred will never cease by hatred. By love alone is it healed. (Nor am I assuming bin Laden is the only guilty party. Hatred itself is.)

RECOMMENDATION

by Thich Nhat Hanh

Promise me
promise me this day,
promise me now,
while the sun is overhead
exactly at the zenith,
promise me.

Even as they
strike you down
with the mountain of hatred and violence;
even as they step on you and crush you
like a worm,
even as they dismember and disembowel you,
remember, brother,
remember:
man is not our enemy.

The only thing worthy of you is compassion—
invincible, limitless, unconditional.
Hatred will never let you face
the beast in man.

One day, when you face this beast alone,
with your courage intact, your eyes kind,
untroubled
(even as no one sees them)
out of your smile
will bloom a flower.
And those who love you
will behold you
across ten thousand worlds of birth and
dying.[3]

Thich Nhat Hanh, beloved Buddhist monk and peace practitioner, wrote this poem in 1965 for the young people he worked with who risked their lives every day during the war in Vietnam. Remember that war? The napalmed naked children fleeing down a flaming road? He wrote it to recommend that they prepare to die without hatred. Some of them had already been killed violently, and he cautioned the others against hating. He told them: "Our enemy is our anger, hatred, greed, fanaticism, and discrimination against (each other). If you die because of violence, you must meditate on compassion in order to forgive those who kill you. When you die realizing this state of compassion, you are truly a child of The Awakened One. Even if you are dying in oppression, shame, and violence, if you can smile with forgiveness, you have great power."

Thich Nhat Hanh reminds us that "When there is a mature relationship between people, there is always compassion and forgiveness." This observation is crucial to how we must now, more than ever, understand our world. Every thought, every act, every gesture, must be in the direction of developing and maintaining a mature relationship with the peoples of the planet; all thought of domination, control, force and violence must be abandoned.

S M

I tell you, Chickadee
I am afraid of people
who cannot cry
Tears left unshed
turn to poison
in the ducts
Ask the next soldier you see
enjoying a massacre
if this is not so.

People who do not cry
are victims
of soul mutilation
paid for in Marlboros
and trucks.

Resist.

Violence does not work
except for the man
who pays your salary
Who knows
if you could still weep
you would not take the job.[4]

As Clarisssa Pinkola Estés, master *contadora* and *curandera*, points out: while it is true that the soul can never be destroyed, it can certainly leave us and take up residence elsewhere. I was struck by how many people I talked to after the bombing of the World Trade Towers and the Pentagon said they were numb. Felt nothing. Or didn't know what to feel. I myself experienced a sensation of hollowness. Emptiness. Insubstantiability. I felt weak, slightly nauseous, and as if my own body were disintegrating. I knew enough to let myself fully feel my feelings, whatever they were. At one point I remember laughing because one of our leaders, perhaps at a loss for something to say and to put a quick us-versus-them spin on the

deeply traumatic events, called the pilots
of the planes going into the Trade Towers
"cowards." It was not a word that came to
my mind at all. In fact, when I watched
the suicide glide of the plane into the sec-
ond tower, what I saw, and instantly recognized, was pain. And desperation. And
disconnection. Alienation. And a closed-
hearted, despairing courage, too, to sacri-
fice one's life (along with the lives of thousands of others) to make a point. What is
the story whose fiery ending I am witness-
ing, I wondered. This was an act by a man
who did not believe, definitely did not
believe, in the possibility of love, or even
common sense, to transform the world. I
can easily imagine there will be thousands
like him born in our time, that from the
roots of this one man's story, they will
come to birth practically every minute;
and our government will not be remotely

38

able to "smoke" all of them "out of their holes." The world being what it is, some of those "holes" are likely to be uncomfortably close to us.

What are we going to feel like, if we kill thousands and thousands of people who somewhat resemble this man? I can tell you: We are not going to feel fine. We are not going to feel happy. Some of us, perhaps the very young, will feel triumphant and larger than life for three weeks or so. After that, we will begin to wonder who exactly it was that we killed. And why. And whether a hungry, naked boy herding goats on a land-mine saturated hill was really the right guy. Murder, after all, is murder, even if it is done in war. It is very intimate. The beings we kill become, somehow, ours for life. Ironically, we become responsible for them in death as we were not in life. With time, we are going to be reminded of a few facts that speak to this: that, for instance, during the Vietnam war, in which America bombed a country many of us up to then had never heard of, fifty thousand Americans died. But since the end of the war over sixty thousand who were in the war have died from suicide and drug over doses and other ailments of the spirit and soul. George Bush, *pére*, counseled us to "put the war (that war) behind us." But as Michael Meade, magical storyteller and warrior, so emphatically reminds us, when speaking of that war, in which he refused to fight: "What is behind us is a long, long row of coffins, and we'd better turn around and genuinely grieve and give our dead, both Vietnamese and American, a proper burial. Then we might be able to talk about going on." It is not too hard to imagine that those who are now calling

for war, so many of them old men, have
not engaged their true feelings in so long
they *think to bomb country after country
is to grieve.*

What grieving is not:

    Grieving is not the same as massacre.

    Grieving is not the same as shopping.

    Grieving is not the same as overeating.

    Grieving is not the same as worrying
about one's weight. (Or one's color, sex or
age.)

    Grieving is not the same as trying to
stay young.

    Grieving is not the same as coloring
your hair a new shade each month to forget you've turned over money that will be
used to blow off people's heads.

    Grieving is not the same as seeing the
shadow in everyone but yourself.

To grieve is above all to acknowledge loss, to understand there is a natural end to endless gain.

To grieve means to come to an understanding, finally, of inevitable balance; Life will right itself, though how it does this remains, and will doubtless remain, mysterious.

The Taliban in Afghanistan, for instance, who have treated the indigenous women with such brutal contempt thousands have been driven to suicide, now face at least a moment in time when theirs is the position of the women they have tortured. It will always be so.

It is this natural balancing of life that we fear; that is why, given the history of our own country, many feel a need to be protected by Star Wars.

At this time of mourning
May we be connected to each other,
May we know the range and depth of feelings
in ourselves and in each other
There is vulnerability, fear, love, rage, hatred,
compassion, courage, despair, and
hope
in ourselves, each other, and the world.
May we know our most authentic feelings
and voice them when we speak,
May we tap into soul and spirit when we are
silent together.
May healing begin in us.
May we form and become a circle.

Begin by holding hands in a circle (even two
people can be a circle)
Be silent and feel the clasp and connection
Of hands and heart.
Then each in turn
Speak for yourself
and listen to each other.
Put judgment aside
Remember that anything voiced that you
want to silence
may be a silenced part of yourself.
Sing what spontaneously wants to be sung
and end each circle as it was begun.
Hold hands once again, hold silence (for med-
itation, contemplation, prayer),
Invite blessings.
Until we meet again.

I received this Rx from Jean Shinoda Bolen, M.D., master healer of the psyche and author of *The Millionth Circle* among many other books. She writes: "A circle is a healing and connecting prescription accessible to everyone. Every family, any group of people anywhere can form one." In preparation for the 5th UN Conference on Women and the United General Assembly Special Session on Children, the Millionth Circle 2005 planning committee wrote this statement of intention: "Circles encourage connection and cooperation among their members and inspire compassionate solutions to individual, community and world problems. We believe that circles support each member to find her or his own voice and to live more courageously. Therefore, we intend to seed and nurture circles, wherever possible, in order to cultivate equality, sustainable livelihoods, preservation of the earth and peace for all. Our aim is to celebrate the millionth circle as the metaphor of an idea whose time has come." The metaphor "the millionth circle" was taken from the title of Jean's book, which in turn was inspired by the story of the "hundredth monkey and morphic field theory" that sustained activists in the 1970-80's in the face of conventional wisdom that said ordinary people could not deter the nuclear arms race.

Jean advises: "Wherever you are today, tomorrow, next week, bring people (include the children) together to form circles. If you are in a group, transform it into a circle, if you are already in a circle, get together. In response to the destruction of buildings, families, lives and everyone's sense of security, this is something you can do to help."

I have been part of a circle for three years. It is one of the most important connections of my life. One reason the circle is so powerful is that it is informed, in fact, shaped by, the Grandmother spirit. The spirit of impartiality, equality, equanimity. Of nurturing but also of fierceness. It has no use for hierarchy. Or patriarchy. It tolerates violence against itself for a while, but will sooner or later rise to defend itself. This is the spirit of the earth itself.

And so today, I feel sent to you, midwives of North America, by the Earth Herself. You are, against the cruelest odds of history and laws, attempting to bring human beings into the world in a way that welcomes them. I have seen your work with my own eyes and I know it is essential in getting human kind back on the right track. Women must be supported, loved, listened to, cared for, as they are carrying life and attempting to deliver it to our world. To us, Life's community, not to the war machine. The child must be able to feel, emerging from the womb, that we are honored it is here. We are thrilled. We are called upon in this frightful time to labor for the body and the soul.

We must learn nothing less than how to be born again.

Just as the body loves exercise, though it complains, the soul loves awareness. For a long time I've pondered the expression "Never let the right hand know what the left hand is doing." This advice, I believe, is wrong. We must struggle to see both our hands, and their activity, clearly. We must see, for instance, the Palestinians and what has happened to their homes, their fields, and their trees; and we must see what is happening to the Israelis and their homes and their fields and their trees. We must see where our tax dollars flow and try, *in awareness*, to follow them. We, as Americans, have a hand in each nation's fate, but we tend to look only at the hand the news media shows us, constantly. This situation in the Middle East, a war between brothers and cousins, may mean the end of life as we in North America know it. It may ultimately mean our lives. The soul wants to know the truth; what is really going on. Nor must we fall asleep while Afghanistan, a country with 700,000 disabled orphans, is being bombed. We must struggle to stay awake enough to imagine what it feels like to be small and afraid, not to have parents, to be disabled, to be hungry and lonely, and not be able, either, to get out of the way of America's wrath. The soul wants to know why we have paid taxes to support the

Taliban. Why, through that group, we have so heartlessly supported the debasement and assassination of The Feminine.

While we trudge onward, trying to remember what Black Elk observed: that all living beings are essentially alike, I recommend the wearing of two threads of different colors, one of them, representing the feminine, red. The red thread should be worn on the left wrist, closest to the heart, and the brown or white or black thread, representing whatever endangers the feminine, the Grandmother, Earth, on the right. These will remind us to stay awake.

It will also help, I think, to create an altar, especially for our children who make up so much of the military. It should be kept beautiful with flowers and candles and bowed to everyday. There is no way most of them will ever understand who they are killing, or why. The souls of many of them will go so far from their bodies during war that they will never return. There should be feathers and stones and other meaningful objects on this altar, but above all, there should be a mirror. And pictures of our loved ones who never knew what struck them on the 11th of September. Together they, our children, and the children our children will kill will create a circle; let us acknowledge that.

While thinking of the Grandmother Spirit that I believe should be guiding Earth, and must, for humans to survive, I thought of three women, all unmarried, as far as I know, two of them childless, all relatively young. Still, they exemplify the spirit of which I speak. They are Julia Butterfly Hill, who sat in a precious, old growth redwood tree for two years trying to save it from being cut down; Amy Goodman, of *Democracy Now*, who has clung to the airwaves to bring us truly informative radio; and Representative Barbara Lee, who alone voted not to give away the Congress's (and therefore the People's) right to declare war. I invoke their names to honor them in this gathering of wise, strong women who will understand exactly how this kind of courage differs from the kind that speaks calmly of "collateral damage" i.e. obliteration of infants, pregnant women and small children, old men running in terror, meted out from the sky.

❧

A mudra is a hand gesture used in meditation to evoke a particular state.

A chant is a repetitive vocalization of one's deepest beliefs and hopes in an effort to inscribe those hopes and beliefs in the courageous and compassionate heart of one's self and others.

<hr/>

On the day of the bombings I realized why Christians cross themselves. And why the people of Islam turn toward Mecca. I knew that I also needed a gesture of self-blessing that would, at the same time, symbolize blessing and protection of the world and its varied inhabitants.

I realized we, as humans, need a New World peace mudra and chant to help us through the days ahead, which will undoubtedly cause unprecedented suffering and pain. Partly because more people than ever before will be conscious of what is happening. And untold thousands will feel completely helpless to do anything about it.

Spirit, the Grandmother Spirit of Earth, sent me this mudra and chant:

The mudra is to hold the thumb and first two fingers together, symbolizing unity, while making a circle around one's heart. A circle that covers as much of the body as possible. Or as large a circle as one has need. This is done three times, while chanting:

One Earth
One People
One Love

One Earth
One People
One Love

One Earth
One People
One Love

Please stand and let us together chant this blessing seven times; seven is the ideal number of people in a circle that is designed to grow the soul and transform the world.

NOTES

1 Constance Webb, *Richard Wright: The Biography of a Major Figure in American Literature.* G. P. Putnam's Sons, 1968.

2 Alice Walker, "The Story of Why I Am Here or A Woman Connects Oppressions; (Putting My Arms Around Sadie Hussein, Age Three)." An address given at a Peace for Cuba Rally, Feb. 1, 1992. In *Anything We Love Can Be Saved, A Writer's Activism,* Random House, 1997.

3 Thich Nhat Hanh, *Call Me By My True Names.* Parallax Press, 1984.

4 Alice Walker, *Horses Make a Landscape Look More Beautiful.* Harcourt Brace Jovanovitch, 1984.

PERMISSIONS

The poem "Recommendation" is reprinted from *Call Me By My True Names: The Collected Poems of Thich Nhat Hanh* (1999) by Thich Nhat Hanh, with permission from Parallax Press, Berkeley, California, www.parallax.org.

"SM" is reprinted from *Horses Make a Landscape Look More Beautiful* (1979) by Alice Walker, with permission from Harcourt Brace Jovanovich.

Excerpt from *Anything We Love Can Be Saved* (1997) by Alice Walker, reprinted with permission from Random House.